CHECKERBOARD BIOGRAPHY LIBRARY

U.S. PRESIDENTS

The United States Presidents

BARACK OBAMA

ABDO Publishing Company

Jill C. Wheeler

visit us at
www.abdopublishing.com

Published by ABDO Publishing Company, 8000 West 78th Street, Edina, Minnesota 55439.
Copyright © 2009 by Abdo Consulting Group, Inc. International copyrights reserved in all
countries. No part of this book may be reproduced in any form without written permission from the
publisher. The Checkerboard Library™ is a trademark and logo of ABDO Publishing Company.

Printed in the United States.

Cover Photo: Public Domain
Interior Photos: AP Images pp. 8, 9, 11, 12, 15, 17, 18, 20, 21, 22, 23, 25, 28; Corbis pp. 5, 13, 29;
    Getty Images pp. 16, 19, 24, 27; iStockphoto p. 32

Editors: Heidi M.D. Elston, Megan M. Gunderson
Art Direction & Cover Design: Neil Klinepier
Interior Design: Jaime Martens

Library of Congress Cataloging-in-Publication Data

Wheeler, Jill C., 1964-
  Barack Obama / Jill C. Wheeler.
      p. cm. -- (The United States presidents)
  Includes index.
  ISBN 978-1-60453-481-8
  1. Obama, Barack--Juvenile literature. 2. Legislators--United States--Biography--Juvenile
literature. 3. African American legislators--United States--Biography--Juvenile literature. 4. United
States. Congress. Senate--Biography--Juvenile literature. 5. Presidential candidates--United States--
Biography--Juvenile literature. 6. Racially mixed people--United States--Biography--Juvenile
literature. I. Title.

  E901.1.O23W49 2009
  973.931092--dc22
  [B]
                                        2008044334

CONTENTS

BARACK OBAMA

On January 20, 2009, Barack Obama took office as the forty-fourth U.S. president. Obama had run his election campaign on a message of change. Millions of voters liked what he had said. His speeches had stirred a sense of excitement and hope.

Critics said Obama did not have enough experience to become president. Yet he had spent many years working as a community organizer. Obama had also served in the Illinois state senate and the U.S. Senate. When he won the long battle to become president, Obama proved his critics wrong.

When he took office, Obama made history. He became the first African-American president of the United States. Many voters hoped he could help America address problems with **discrimination**. Americans also hoped President Obama would help the country's two major political parties work together.

TIMELINE

1961 - On August 4, Barack Hussein Obama Jr. was born in Honolulu, Hawaii.

1983 - Obama graduated from Columbia University in New York City, New York.

1985 - Obama moved to Chicago, Illinois, where he began working as a community organizer.

1988 - Obama entered Harvard Law School in Cambridge, Massachusetts.

1990 - Obama became the first African-American president of the *Harvard Law Review*.

1991 - Obama graduated with honors from Harvard Law School.

1992 - Obama married Michelle LaVaughn Robinson; he began teaching at the University of Chicago; Obama led Illinois Project VOTE.

1995 - *Dreams from My Father: A Story of Race and Inheritance* was published.

1996 - Obama was elected to the Illinois state senate.

1998 - Obama's daughter Malia Ann was born.

2001 - Obama's daughter Natasha, called Sasha, was born.

2004 - Obama gave a speech at the Democratic National Convention in Boston, Massachusetts; he won election to the U.S. Senate.

2007 - In February, Obama announced he would run for U.S. president.

2008 - On August 23, Obama chose Joe Biden as his running mate; Obama officially became the Democratic nominee for U.S. president on August 27; on November 4, Obama defeated John McCain to win the presidential election.

2009 - On January 20, Obama took office as the forty-fourth U.S. president.

DID YOU KNOW?

On their first date, Barack Obama took Michelle to the Art Institute of Chicago in Illinois.

Obama has written two best-selling books. *Dreams from My Father: A Story of Race and Inheritance* was published in 1995. *The Audacity of Hope: Thoughts on Reclaiming the American Dream* followed in 2006.

The 2006 Grammy Award for Spoken Word Album went to Obama. He won for the audio recording of *Dreams from My Father*. Obama won the same award in 2008 for *The Audacity of Hope*.

ISLAND YOUTH

Barack Hussein Obama Jr. was born on August 4, 1961, in Honolulu, Hawaii. He was named after his father. The name *Barack* means "blessed" in the Swahili language. When he was young, Barack went by Barry.

Barack Obama Sr. was from Alego, Kenya. He was a member of the Luo tribe in Africa. In 1959, he became the first African student to attend the University of Hawaii in Honolulu. Barry's mother was Stanley Ann Dunham. She went by the name Ann.

Barry's parents met in a Russian language class at the University of Hawaii.

FAST FACTS

BORN - August 4, 1961
WIFE - Michelle LaVaughn Robinson (1964–)
CHILDREN - 2
POLITICAL PARTY - Democrat
AGE AT INAUGURATION - 47
YEARS SERVED - 2009–
VICE PRESIDENT - Joe Biden

Ann grew up in Kansas, California, Texas, and Washington. She met Barack Sr. while attending the University of Hawaii.

When Barry was just two, his father moved to Cambridge, Massachusetts. There, he attended Harvard University. Ann and Barry stayed behind in Hawaii.

A few years later, Barry's parents divorced. His father then returned to Kenya. There, he worked for the government as an **economist**.

Young Barry

INDONESIA

Barry's mother soon remarried. His stepfather, Lolo Soetoro, was from Indonesia. When Barry was six, he and his mother joined Lolo in Jakarta, Indonesia.

Young Barry found Indonesia to be very different from Hawaii. The roads were not paved. His home had no electricity. And chickens, baby crocodiles, and brightly colored birds lived in his backyard!

In Indonesia, most foreign students attended the International School. However, Barry's family could not afford to send him there. So, he attended a Catholic school and a public school instead.

Ann worried Barry wasn't being challenged enough in school. So, she woke him up at 4:00 AM every morning. Then, she taught him English lessons from a **correspondence course**.

By age ten, Barry had finished all the lessons from his correspondence course. So, his mother decided he should continue

Barry with his stepfather, mother, and half sister Maya

his education in America. Barry returned to Hawaii to live with his
mother's parents. With their help, he earned a **scholarship** to
attend Punahou School in Honolulu.

HAWAIIAN EDUCATION

Punahou was the most prestigious **preparatory school** in Hawaii. Barry was one of only a few African-American students at the school. He felt different because he had a white mother and a black father. Barry felt torn between two worlds.

Barry only saw his father for about a month when he was ten. In 1982, Barack Sr. was killed in a car accident in Kenya.

When Barry was in middle school, Barack Sr. returned to Hawaii to visit. This was the most time young Barry would have with his father.

Barry's mother also came back to Hawaii. There, she continued her education. When Barry was 14, his mother was ready to return to Indonesia. But, Barry was tired of being the new kid in school. So, he decided to stay in Hawaii with his grandparents.

Barry did not always do well in school. He preferred basketball and bodysurfing to studying. Yet Barry was very smart. He could write a successful paper the night before it was due! Barry graduated from high school with **honors** in 1979.

Barry with his grandparents

DISCOVERING CHANGE

After high school, Obama moved to Los Angeles, California. There, he attended Occidental College from 1979 to 1981. While in college, Obama began to get involved in social issues. He gave a speech at Occidental about problems in South Africa. At that moment, he realized that words could be powerful tools for change.

After two years, Obama transferred to Columbia University in New York City, New York. At Columbia, he studied **political science**. Obama also continued noticing how racial differences affect communities. He grew convinced that **activism** was important to bring about change.

Obama graduated from Columbia in 1983. After graduation, he spent one year working in finance. At the same time, he began looking for a job in community service. Obama sent out letters across the United States asking what he could do to help. Only one of the groups he wrote to responded. Soon, Obama was headed to Chicago, Illinois.

At Columbia University, Obama began going by Barack instead of Barry.

COMMUNITY ORGANIZER

In 1985, Obama moved to Chicago. There, he worked for the Calumet Community Religious Conference. On Chicago's South Side, many people had lost jobs in the steel industry. Obama's organization helped create ways for these people to find new jobs.

Obama's work also took him to the Altgeld Gardens housing project. Part of his job was to listen to the people living there tell their stories. In this way, he learned about the problems they faced. Obama then helped the residents become involved in improving their own community.

Obama helped Altgeld Gardens residents work to make their community safer.

Obama never stopped believing in the power of community involvement.
It became a key idea during his presidential campaign.

Obama enjoyed his work as a community organizer. Yet he
wanted more. Obama believed community involvement could
improve lives. But, he felt that laws and politics must also change.
So after three years, Obama returned to school to study law.

LAW SCHOOL

In 1988, Obama entered Harvard Law School in Cambridge, Massachusetts. He was a very successful student. Obama showed strong leadership as well as good writing and editing skills. He also displayed an ability to see both sides of an issue. So in 1990, he was elected president of the *Harvard Law Review*. Obama was the first African American to hold this position.

In this role, Obama was responsible for the journal's 80 editors. With Obama in charge, writers with different beliefs knew they would have a voice. Obama graduated with **honors** from Harvard Law School in 1991.

In 104 years, the Harvard Law Review *had never had an African-American president.*

Michelle Obama with Sasha (left) *and Malia*

Two summers earlier, Obama had worked at the Sidley Austin LLP law firm in Chicago. There, he met Harvard Law School graduate Michelle LaVaughn Robinson. The two stayed in touch when Obama returned to Harvard.

After graduation, Obama moved back to Chicago. This was Michelle's childhood home. She and Obama married in 1992 and had two daughters. Malia Ann was born in 1998. Natasha, called Sasha, was born in 2001.

BACK TO CHICAGO

Back in Illinois, Obama began teaching **constitutional** law at the University of Chicago. He worked there from 1992 to 2004. Meanwhile, Obama was also working for the Miner, Barnhill and Galland law firm. There, he focused on **civil rights** issues.

Obama was a professor at the University of Chicago Law School.

Obama worked on housing and employment **discrimination** cases. And, he helped with voting rights cases.

At the same time, Obama did not give up on community organizing. He served on the boards of the Woods Fund and the Joyce Foundation. These groups gave money to community organizations.

Also in 1992, Obama led Illinois Project VOTE. This organization worked to get more African Americans involved in the election process. Obama's efforts helped register more than 100,000 voters.

Obama had been gaining national attention since law school. This earned him an offer to write a book. Obama wrote about his life story and his struggles with racial identity. This became *Dreams from My Father: A Story of Race and Inheritance*. The book was published in 1995.

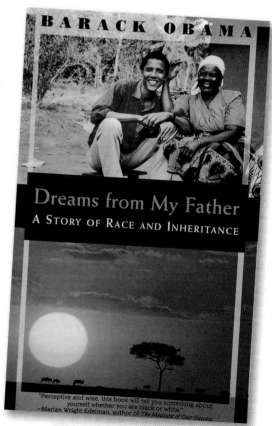

ENTERING POLITICS

After Illinois Project VOTE, Obama did not stop working in politics. In 1996, he ran for the Illinois state senate as a **Democrat**. Many people in the community knew of him and his work. So, Obama won the election!

In the state senate, Obama was chairman of the Public Health and Welfare Committee. He worked to increase funding for the prevention and treatment of **AIDS**. He also worked to reduce racial **profiling**.

Senator Obama helped pass the Earned Income Tax Credit. This provided tax cuts for Illinois families. He also worked to expand early childhood education. Obama became known as someone who could work with both Democrats and **Republicans**.

Bobby Rush began serving in the U.S. House of Representatives in 1993.

22

In the 2000 primary election, Obama received half as many votes as Rush.

In 2000, Obama tried to win a seat in the U.S. House of Representatives. At the time, **Democrat** Bobby Rush held the seat. During the **primary**, Obama lost to Rush.

U.S. SENATOR

In 2004, Obama ran for the U.S. Senate. He easily won the **Democratic primary** for the seat. Even Rush supported him!

Republicans chose Alan Keyes to run for the Senate. However, Keyes had recently moved from Maryland in order to run. He also said a number of things that upset some voters.

Obama's race against Keyes marked the first time both the Democratic and Republican nominees for a Senate seat were African-American.

In November, Obama easily won the election. He took office on January 3, 2005. At the time, he was the only African-American U.S. senator. And, he was only the fifth African-American senator in U.S. history.

In the Senate, Obama quickly got to work. He served on both the Foreign Relations and **Veterans** Affairs committees. Obama also served on the **Environment** and **Public Works** Committee. And, Senator Obama was an early opponent of the **Iraq War**.

On the Foreign Relations Committee, Obama worked with his future running mate, Joe Biden (standing, center). *He also served with 2004 presidential candidate John Kerry* (far left).

THE 2008 CAMPAIGN

During his Senate campaign, Obama had gained national attention. He had given a speech at the 2004 **Democratic National Convention** in Boston, Massachusetts. His speaking skills left his audience impressed. Immediately, people began asking Obama if he planned to run for president.

In February 2007, Obama announced his candidacy for president. He joined a large group of **Democratic** candidates. Obama's main opponents were Senator Hillary Clinton and former senator John Edwards. Both were better known than Obama. And, both had more political experience.

The campaign trail was long and challenging. On January 3, 2008, Obama won the Iowa **caucus**. Then five days later, he failed to win the New Hampshire **primary**.

By February 2008, the field of candidates had narrowed to Obama and Clinton. Primary wins went back and forth between the two candidates for months. Finally on June 7, Clinton announced her support for Obama.

Obama announced his candidacy for president at the Old State Capitol in Springfield, Illinois. In 1858, Abraham Lincoln had given a speech there announcing his run for the U.S. Senate. Lincoln later became president.

PRESIDENT OBAMA

Next, Obama had to choose a **running mate**. On August 23, he picked Senator Joe Biden of Delaware to run for vice president. Biden had a long political career. He had served in the U.S. Senate since 1973. And like Obama, he served on the Foreign Relations Committee. Biden brought much political experience to the ticket.

On August 27, Obama became the **Democratic** Party's official nominee for president. Then he faced off against his **Republican** opponent, Senator John McCain of Arizona. McCain chose Alaska governor Sarah Palin as his running mate.

Obama and McCain ran tough campaigns. Voters looked to them for answers about the American **economy** and the **Iraq War**. The race remained close.

John McCain and Sarah Palin

Joe Biden and Barack Obama

Then on November 4, 2008, Barack Obama was elected the forty-fourth president of the United States. He took office on January 20, 2009. With this, he became the first African-American president in U.S. history. President Obama promised change and gave Americans hope for the future.

OFFICE OF THE PRESIDENT

BRANCHES OF GOVERNMENT

The U.S. government is divided into three branches. They are the executive, legislative, and judicial branches. This division is called a separation of powers. Each branch has some power over the others. This is called a system of checks and balances.

EXECUTIVE BRANCH

The executive branch enforces laws. It is made up of the president, the vice president, and the president's cabinet. The president represents the United States around the world. He or she oversees relations with other countries and signs treaties. The president signs bills into law and appoints officials and federal judges. He or she also leads the military and manages government workers.

LEGISLATIVE BRANCH

The legislative branch makes laws, maintains the military, and regulates trade. It also has the power to declare war. This branch consists of the Senate and the House of Representatives. Together, these two houses make up Congress. Each state has two senators. A state's population determines the number of representatives it has.

JUDICIAL BRANCH

The judicial branch interprets laws. It consists of district courts, courts of appeals, and the Supreme Court. District courts try cases. If a person disagrees with a trial's outcome, he or she may appeal. If the courts of appeals support the ruling, a person may appeal to the Supreme Court. The Supreme Court also makes sure that laws follow the U.S. Constitution.

QUALIFICATIONS FOR OFFICE

To be president, a person must meet three requirements. A candidate must be at least 35 years old and a natural-born U.S. citizen. He or she must also have lived in the United States for at least 14 years.

ELECTORAL COLLEGE

The U.S. presidential election is an indirect election. Voters from each state choose electors to represent them in the Electoral College. The number of electors from each state is based on population. Each elector has one electoral vote. Electors are pledged to cast their vote for the candidate who receives the highest number of popular votes in their state. A candidate must receive the majority of Electoral College votes to win.

TERM OF OFFICE

Each president may be elected to two four-year terms. Sometimes, a president may only be elected once. This happens if he or she served more than two years of the previous president's term.

The presidential election is held on the Tuesday after the first Monday in November. The president is sworn in on January 20 of the following year. At that time, he or she takes the oath of office:

I do solemnly swear (or affirm) that I will faithfully execute the office of President of the United States, and will to the best of my ability, preserve, protect and defend the Constitution of the United States.

LINE OF SUCCESSION

The Presidential Succession Act of 1947 defines who becomes president if the president cannot serve. The vice president is first in the line of succession. Next are the Speaker of the House and the President Pro Tempore of the Senate. If none of these individuals is able to serve, the office falls to the president's cabinet members. They would take office in the order in which each department was created:

Secretary of State

Secretary of the Treasury

Secretary of Defense

Attorney General

Secretary of the Interior

Secretary of Agriculture

Secretary of Commerce

Secretary of Labor

Secretary of Health and Human Services

Secretary of Housing and Urban Development

Secretary of Transportation

Secretary of Energy

Secretary of Education

Secretary of Veterans Affairs

Secretary of Homeland Security

Benefits

• While in office, the president receives a salary of $400,000 each year. He or she lives in the White House and has 24-hour Secret Service protection.

• The president may travel on a Boeing 747 jet called Air Force One. The airplane can accommodate 70 passengers. It has kitchens, a dining room, sleeping areas, and a conference room. It also has fully equipped offices with the latest communications systems. Air Force One can fly halfway around the world before needing to refuel. It can even refuel in flight!

• If the president wishes to travel by car, he or she uses Cadillac One. Cadillac One is a Cadillac Deville. It has been modified with heavy armor and communications systems. The president takes Cadillac One along when visiting other countries if secure transportation will be needed.

• The president also travels on a helicopter called Marine One. Like the presidential car, Marine One accompanies the president when traveling abroad if necessary.

• Sometimes, the president needs to get away and relax with family and friends. Camp David is the official presidential retreat. It is located in the cool, wooded mountains in Maryland. The U.S. Navy maintains the retreat, and the U.S. Marine Corps keeps it secure. The camp offers swimming, tennis, golf, and hiking.

• When the president leaves office, he or she receives Secret Service protection for ten more years. He or she also receives a yearly pension of $191,300 and funding for office space, supplies, and staff.

PRESIDENTS AND THEIR TERMS

PRESIDENT	PARTY	TOOK OFFICE	LEFT OFFICE	TERMS SERVED	VICE PRESIDENT
George Washington	None	April 30, 1789	March 4, 1797	Two	John Adams
John Adams	Federalist	March 4, 1797	March 4, 1801	One	Thomas Jefferson
Thomas Jefferson	Democratic-Republican	March 4, 1801	March 4, 1809	Two	Aaron Burr, George Clinton
James Madison	Democratic-Republican	March 4, 1809	March 4, 1817	Two	George Clinton, Elbridge Gerry
James Monroe	Democratic-Republican	March 4, 1817	March 4, 1825	Two	Daniel D. Tompkins
John Quincy Adams	Democratic-Republican	March 4, 1825	March 4, 1829	One	John C. Calhoun
Andrew Jackson	Democrat	March 4, 1829	March 4, 1837	Two	John C. Calhoun, Martin Van Buren
Martin Van Buren	Democrat	March 4, 1837	March 4, 1841	One	Richard M. Johnson
William H. Harrison	Whig	March 4, 1841	April 4, 1841	Died During First Term	John Tyler
John Tyler	Whig	April 6, 1841	March 4, 1845	Completed Harrison's Term	Office Vacant
James K. Polk	Democrat	March 4, 1845	March 4, 1849	One	George M. Dallas
Zachary Taylor	Whig	March 5, 1849	July 9, 1850	Died During First Term	Millard Fillmore

PRESIDENTS 1–12, 1789–1850

PRESIDENT	PARTY	TOOK OFFICE	LEFT OFFICE	TERMS SERVED	VICE PRESIDENT
Millard Fillmore	Whig	July 10, 1850	March 4, 1853	Completed Taylor's Term	Office Vacant
Franklin Pierce	Democrat	March 4, 1853	March 4, 1857	One	William R.D. King
James Buchanan	Democrat	March 4, 1857	March 4, 1861	One	John C. Breckinridge
Abraham Lincoln	Republican	March 4, 1861	April 15, 1865	Served One Term, Died During Second Term	Hannibal Hamlin, Andrew Johnson
Andrew Johnson	Democrat	April 15, 1865	March 4, 1869	Completed Lincoln's Second Term	Office Vacant
Ulysses S. Grant	Republican	March 4, 1869	March 4, 1877	Two	Schuyler Colfax, Henry Wilson
Rutherford B. Hayes	Republican	March 3, 1877	March 4, 1881	One	William A. Wheeler
James A. Garfield	Republican	March 4, 1881	September 19, 1881	Died During First Term	Chester Arthur
Chester Arthur	Republican	September 20, 1881	March 4, 1885	Completed Garfield's Term	Office Vacant
Grover Cleveland	Democrat	March 4, 1885	March 4, 1889	One	Thomas A. Hendricks
Benjamin Harrison	Republican	March 4, 1889	March 4, 1893	One	Levi P. Morton
Grover Cleveland	Democrat	March 4, 1893	March 4, 1897	One	Adlai E. Stevenson
William McKinley	Republican	March 4, 1897	September 14, 1901	Served One Term, Died During Second Term	Garret A. Hobart, Theodore Roosevelt

PRESIDENT	PARTY	TOOK OFFICE	LEFT OFFICE	TERMS SERVED	VICE PRESIDENT
Theodore Roosevelt	Republican	September 14, 1901	March 4, 1909	Completed McKinley's Second Term, Served One Term	Office Vacant, Charles Fairbanks
William Taft	Republican	March 4, 1909	March 4, 1913	One	James S. Sherman
Woodrow Wilson	Democrat	March 4, 1913	March 4, 1921	Two	Thomas R. Marshall
Warren G. Harding	Republican	March 4, 1921	August 2, 1923	Died During First Term	Calvin Coolidge
Calvin Coolidge	Republican	August 3, 1923	March 4, 1929	Completed Harding's Term, Served One Term	Office Vacant, Charles Dawes
Herbert Hoover	Republican	March 4, 1929	March 4, 1933	One	Charles Curtis
Franklin D. Roosevelt	Democrat	March 4, 1933	April 12, 1945	Served Three Terms, Died During Fourth Term	John Nance Garner, Henry A. Wallace, Harry S. Truman
Harry S. Truman	Democrat	April 12, 1945	January 20, 1953	Completed Roosevelt's Fourth Term, Served One Term	Office Vacant, Alben Barkley
Dwight D. Eisenhower	Republican	January 20, 1953	January 20, 1961	Two	Richard Nixon
John F. Kennedy	Democrat	January 20, 1961	November 22, 1963	Died During First Term	Lyndon B. Johnson
Lyndon B. Johnson	Democrat	November 22, 1963	January 20, 1969	Completed Kennedy's Term, Served One Term	Office Vacant, Hubert H. Humphrey
Richard Nixon	Republican	January 20, 1969	August 9, 1974	Completed First Term, Resigned During Second Term	Spiro T. Agnew, Gerald Ford

PRESIDENT	PARTY	TOOK OFFICE	LEFT OFFICE	TERMS SERVED	VICE PRESIDENT
Gerald Ford	Republican	August 9, 1974	January 20, 1977	Completed Nixon's Second Term	Nelson A. Rockefeller
Jimmy Carter	Democrat	January 20, 1977	January 20, 1981	One	Walter Mondale
Ronald Reagan	Republican	January 20, 1981	January 20, 1989	Two	George H.W. Bush
George H.W. Bush	Republican	January 20, 1989	January 20, 1993	One	Dan Quayle
Bill Clinton	Democrat	January 20, 1993	January 20, 2001	Two	Al Gore
George W. Bush	Republican	January 20, 2001	January 20, 2009	Two	Dick Cheney
Barack Obama	Democrat	January 20, 2009			Joe Biden

"Change happens because the American people demand it - because they rise up and insist on new ideas and new leadership, a new politics for a new time." Barack Obama

WRITE TO THE PRESIDENT

You may write to the president at:

**The White House
1600 Pennsylvania Avenue NW
Washington, DC 20500**

You may e-mail the president at:

comments@whitehouse.gov

GLOSSARY

activism - a practice that emphasizes direct action in support of or in opposition to an issue that causes disagreement.

AIDS - Acquired Immune Deficiency Syndrome. A disease that weakens the immune system. It is caused by the Human Immunodeficiency Virus (HIV).

caucus - a meeting held by members of a certain political party to nominate candidates for public office and decide on party policy.

civil rights - the individual rights of a citizen, such as the right to vote or freedom of speech.

constitutional - something relating to or following the laws of a constitution. A constitution is the laws that govern a country or a state.

correspondence course - a class given by mail instead of in a classroom.

Democrat - a member of the Democratic political party. Democrats believe in social change and strong government.

Democratic National Convention - a national meeting held every four years during which the Democratic Party chooses its candidates for president and vice president.

discrimination (dihs-krih-muh-NAY-shuhn) - unfair treatment based on factors such as a person's race, religion, or gender.

economy - the way a nation uses its money, goods, and natural resources. An economist is a person who is an expert in this.

environment - all the surroundings that affect the growth and well-being of a living thing.

honors - special credit given to a student for above-average work.

Iraq War - a conflict begun in March 2003 when the United States and its allies invaded Iraq. After the fall of the Iraqi government, U.S. troops remained in Iraq to help stabilize the new government.

political science - the study of government and politics.

preparatory school - a typically private school that prepares students for college.

primary - a method of selecting candidates to run for public office. A political party holds an election among its own members to select the party members who will represent it in the coming general election.

profiling - the act of suspecting or targeting a person based on behavior or observed characteristics, such as race.

public works - projects the government pays for, such as roads, dams, or sewers.

Republican - a member of the Republican political party. Republicans are conservative and believe in small government.

running mate - a candidate running for a lower-rank position on an election ticket, especially the candidate for vice president.

scholarship - a gift of money to help a student pay for instruction.

veteran - a person who has served in the armed forces.

WEB SITES

To learn more about Barack Obama, visit ABDO Publishing Company on the World Wide Web at **www.abdopublishing.com**. Web sites about Barack Obama are featured on our Book Links page. These links are routinely monitored and updated to provide the most current information available.

INDEX